21-Day
Transformation Journey
"Daily Lessons for Your Soul"

Towanda McEachern

DEDICATION

This workbook is dedicated to 'YOU' because it's time to get out of your own way.

CONTENTS

ACKNOWLEDGMENTS

During this process of writing, my husband, Roger and my youngest daughter, Kayla kept me on point. They made sure that I was working on what I said I was committed to and would always check in with me to see what day I was working on. I love you guys and thank you for supporting me.

I'm grateful for my business coach, who has helped me to see the possibility of what could be and has encouraged, supported and held me accountable along the way. Thank you Winston ☺.

What started out as an email has morphed into this great teaching tool, and every step of the way there was one person who would send me their thoughts daily. What they didn't know was they were my gauge, and they were leading me in the right direction. They were on the journey with me. As I wrote each day, they were giving me direction through feedback. Thank you Errica Quartey; now it's your turn. I've left a trail of breadcrumbs for you.

I want to thank my sister, Nicole Jones who is also my editor. She has been a teacher for over 12+ years; and she always tells me I write how I speak, duh… It just sounds better. (Now don't edit that, lol) She is also one of my biggest cheerleaders. She was one of the first people to believe in me when I didn't believe in myself. She saw me before I saw myself. I will always love you.

To my oldest daughter, Kari' you have and will always be one of my biggest inspirations. I love your life ☺.

A few tips to help you on this journey.

1. The 21 days will act as a tour guide. It is not designed to overwhelm you.
2. Your 21 days may not be consecutive. It may be Monday through Friday. It's ok. Do what works for you.
3. Try to find a quiet place to sit and read.
4. Take time to answer the questions. Answering the questions give you an opportunity to reflect.
5. Understand healing is a process. Allow the journey to lead you.
6. Share the journey with a friend.

Day 1

UNDER CONSTRUCTION

They say the definition of insanity is doing the same thing while expecting a different result. Well, I think I went insane a long time ago. The problem is I'm in good company. We say we want things to change, but we keep doing the same things over and over again. I look at society as a whole and I see many things and issues that need to change. Sometimes I wonder, "Does anyone else see this or have we just become numb to it?" I figured I would take a crack at this thing to see what I could come up with. This is my attempt to add value and make a contribution to society. I believe we are supposed to contribute to society, for the most part, people really do want to contribute.

Everyone has something to say, but no one wants to go first. Well, I'll just raise my hand and I'll go first. Today's devotion is entitled "Under Construction" because that's what I believe needs to happen.

When a building is not suited for its intended use, it has to be reconstructed or demolished. Sometimes tearing it down is a lot better than trying to reconstruct it.

But in life, we can't just demolish a person we have to go through a transformation or a restoration. Let's start by putting up a sign so other's will know what's about to take place "Under Construction" . The sign gives a warning of what is taking place. I think maybe it's time our lives went under a little construction. Maybe somewhere along the way something happened to our foundation. Maybe it got cracked or possibly it was constructed that way from birth. Yes, from birth. Sometimes we are born with things that are out of our control, or maybe along the way life began to eat at your foundation and it began to erode and crack.

I used to work for a developer so I understand a little about the process of what it takes to build a home from the ground up. For example; footings, plumbing, electrical lines, foundation, framing, insulation, sheetrock, walls, doors, paint, cabinet installation, light fixtures, electrical outlets, appliances, there is so much that goes into it. In order to make sure the project runs smoothly and add a level of accountability there is a Project Manager. The Project Manager oversees the process and makes sure the project is on task according to the specs and budget. During the 21 day Journey, I will be acting as your Project Manager in the form of your Transformation Coach.

Let the Journey Begin...

As you go on this journey, take a moment to evaluate where you are in your life. (Tell the truth, this only works if you are honest with yourself.)

Food For Thought

You want something different, you have to do something different.

Under Construction

Where are you on this journey? Do an evaluation of following areas of your life.

Mentally-

Emotionally-

Spiritually-

After reading today's lesson, what did you hear?

What are you going to do with the new information you received?

My thoughts… Use this space to write your "Aha" Moments?

DAY 2

A STAR IS BORN

Your life is about so much more than you think. There is a big picture and you have been invited to play a major role in it. Most of the time, people can't see how they could possibly fit in the picture with all the junk in their lives, thinking about where they came from and especially what's going on in their lives now. What we don't understand is that all of those things are precisely why you have been cast in that role. No one else can play this part except you. Your personality, character and life experiences are all the dynamics that are needed to play the role. There are foundational things you have to do to ready yourself. You must actively prepare yourself for this role. You are the STAR in the role of your LIFE.

Think about your life; where you were born, who your parents are, your siblings and your entire family make up. It was not an accident.

We must stop playing the blame game; we blame our parents, society, government, police, school, everyone except ourselves. I know there are things that have happened to you that were not your fault and you were left to deal with the aftermath of it. But, how we respond is key. Now that you have gone through that situation, ask yourself- what do I need to do to pick myself up and begin the healing process so I can move forward with my life?

What we tend to do is when something happens to us, we tend to get stuck and sometimes we check out. We create these mental roadblocks and barriers that prevent us from moving forward. We replay it over and over in our heads until it becomes etched in our soul and we become one with it. I'm not negating or downplaying what has happened to you. Trust me I have had my fair share of trauma, but what has happened to you is not the sum total of who you are. It's what you do with it that defines you. How do you allow those broken pieces to serve you? How do you begin to heal and possibly help someone else heal from similar situations?

If we self-govern and introspect we would begin to see a different perspective that would cause us to take a different approach to life. We could shift from victim to VICTOR!!

In life, there are many circumstances that are going to come your way. How you respond and grow pass them is going to be a real testament to the content of your character. Learning to forgive is a key element to your healing. Moving past your pain is the key to knowing how to live your life and allowing your pain to turn into PURPOSE!

Food For Thought

Denial
is not a form of
therapy,
you must deal
so you can
heal.

A Star is Born

What dynamics are needed to play the staring role of your life?

When something happens to us and we get stuck what do we create?

Name 2 key elements to healing.

After reading today's lesson, what did you hear?

What are you going to do with the new information you received?

My thoughts… Use this space to write your "Aha" Moments?

DAY 3

TOXIC LOGIC

It's all in your head. For years I've been wondering why I wasn't moving forward and why I would seemingly continue to talk myself in and out of things before I would really even start them. I would get a good idea, go through all of its greatness and its full potential, and by the next day, I would have talked myself out of it within a matter of seconds. Toxic logic is when you keep talking yourself in and out of something before it even starts.

I realized that the birthing place had also become the burial place. It was where the dreams were born and where they died. The emotions of it all were tangled together creating mixed emotions. That's why it's important to act quickly. If you don't the birthing place will become the burial place all in one shot.

Toxic Logic can cause your ideas to be stillborn; meaning you went through the birthing process and when the idea was birthed it came out dead. It was dead before it even had a chance to live. It's not real until you make it real. Your thoughts are just that; thoughts. There is an old proverb that says, "Watch your thoughts, they become your words, watch your words they become your actions, watch your actions, they become your habits, watch your habits, they become your destiny." Thoughts can turn into something if you allow it to. So many times we kill it before we even allow it to manifest. The fear of failure is all in your mind. It's you playing out every negative scenario and it frightens you. You feel the emotions as if it has already happened. The problem is-It's not REAL. I heard fear as an acronym meaning False Evidence Appearing Real.

The problem with this is your subconscious doesn't know what's real and what's fake. For years you have been talking yourself out of things because of fear. Now, I'm not saying you shouldn't weigh your options about a decision and contemplate the pros and cons. Don't allow it to paralyze you. Yes, look at the facts, but also you need to trust God and have faith that he will lead you in the right direction.

We have wasted so much of our lives with this toxic logic that it has robbed us of so many unproductive years. We could have been producing, instead, we were crying when we could have been REJOICING.

Give your dreams a chance...

Food For Thought

A renewed mind is a free mind. Lean not on your own understanding.

Toxic Logic

What is "Toxic Logic"?

What happens when you don't act quickly?

What is the acronym for FEAR?

After reading today's lesson, what did you hear?

What are you going to do with the new information you received?

My thoughts… Use this space to write your "Aha" Moments?

DAY 4

YOU CAN DO IT

When trying to bring your vision to pass, at first it may seem like an impossible task, fear and uncertainty will start to kick in. Let me be the first to say YOU REALLY CAN DO IT! I know you're afraid of the unknown and yes it can be frightening. Charting unknown territories even with a plan is still not a guarantee. I know what it's like to have a vision and It looks one-way in your head but you are not sure of the final outcome. Trust me I understand. Before many of my projects get underway I would talk myself out of it before I ever started.

Faith and fear can not occupy the same space I had to learn to make a conscious and deliberate decision to allow my faith to take over. I had to start thinking with the end in mind and work my way towards the vision. I knew I wanted my life to change and I couldn't allow myself to keep doing the same things. I wanted different results so I had to change something in the equation. I had to change ME. I had to change my walk, my talk, my perspective and I had to develop a laser focus mindset and get clear about what I wanted. I had to silence the naysayers, and I truly had to silence the capital naysayer; ME.

When it was all said and done there was no one standing in my way telling me I couldn't do it EXCEPT me. Having people around you who believe in you until you can believe in yourself is key. Sometimes you need to borrow their vision and see what they see in you in order to catapult you to where you need to go. That's why it's important who you surround yourself with. It's important to guard who you allow to have access in your life.

Your purpose and your passion will keep calling you night and day. You awake to it and you go to sleep to it. You dream of it all the time, but you have to develop a system and a plan to bring it to fruition. A dream without action is just that; a DREAM. I remember I use to try and convince myself if I do little things it would add up. The problem with doing little things is that it takes longer to build momentum. Once you've made a deliberate, conscious decision it's best to take massive action so you can see massive results and then be consistent with it.

The longer you sit around not answering the call, the more zeal you are losing. When purposes are stagnated it leads to frustration. Don't frustrate your purpose it leads to an unhappy, unfulfilled life.

So, what are you waiting for? YOU CAN DO IT!!

Food For Thought

Massive action produces massive results.

You Can Do It!

In order to be clear about what you want, what has to change?

What must you develop in order to bring your dreams to fruition?

What leads to frustration?

After reading today's lesson, what did you hear?

What are you going to do with the new information you received?

My thoughts… Use this space to write your "Aha" Moments?

DAY 5

STAND IN IT

Our truth is relative to where we are in life. You will find that what was true for you at one point in your life may not be true at another point. Truth is not like a math problem, where it either is or it isn't. Assessing where you are in life is a big part of standing in your truth. It is essential to your growth and development. Truth is also relative to the information you have at that moment. New information can alter what you know or believe to be true.

Tell yourself the truth about where you are at this moment. Not your truth in comparison to someone else's life because what you are seeing may not be the whole truth. I remember when a picture was worth a thousand words and we would believe it if we saw it. That is no longer the case; social media and Photoshop have changed the dynamics of how we see things. What we see is sometimes only part of it.

Ownership and taking responsibility for your actions are paramount in standing in your truth. Your morals, your values, and your integrity are part of your characteristics in determining how you will operate daily and what governs your life. We all have a set of rules that we live by. Right or wrong there are things we believe and we hold true to them. When thinking of this, one of the things that came to my mind was the code of the streets regarding snitching. Even if something was seen, some people have developed a model and creed they live by that says we can't tell you what we saw, even if we know. It doesn't matter if you don't live by it, it still stands true for some people.

The truth is it's about taking stock of the inventory in your heart. Knowing where you are will help you determine where you need to go. Before you set your GPS to take you somewhere it asked you do you want to use your current location it cannot guide you if it doesn't know where to start. When we are referring to the GPS we tend to think with the end in mind, our destination. But your starting point is just as important; that's where I want us to begin. Before you plan to go on any journey you need to make plans and prepare for the journey. No one takes a road trip without first properly assessing if they are equipped for the journey.

You should begin your day with a daily assessment. It will help keep you grounded and on task. Knowing if you are properly equipped or what else you need is a wise move to make before you begin the journey.

Food For Thought

Allow your TRUTH to evolve and be sure to GROW with it.

Stand in it

When you have new information, what can it do?

What is paramount for standing in your truth?

How should you begin your day?

After reading today's lesson, what did you hear?

What are you going to do with the new information you received?

My thoughts… Use this space to write your "Aha" Moments?

DAY 6

THE ASSESSMENT

Each day during this journey you will unpack information that will expound one upon the other. As a result, it will be etched in the embodiment of who you are so much that if you apply them to your life you will have no other choice but to SUCCEED. That is the GOAL.

It's time to tear down the walls and barriers that you have built in order to move forward. There is a wall that you have wedged between you and the life you know you were born to live. Each of us has God-given gifts, talents and abilities. Those gifts are to be used to carry out a specific mission in life. You hold a piece to a puzzle that is much bigger than you. You are NECESSARY, without your piece the puzzle is not complete.

Knowing where you are can help you understand where you are going.

The prefix re- means "again" or "backward". I heard someone say that life is lived forward, but you learn it backwards; they say hindsight is 20/20. Well, if that's the case why not use your hindsight to propel you forward. It's a matter of extracting from the experiences you've had in life and allowing them to serve you in the form of lessons. Whenever you are going to shoot a bow and arrow, you have to pull the arrow back in order to propel it forward. The further you pull it back the further it will shoot forward.

The big RE...

Let's clarify where you are on this journey. You will find yourself at one of 3 stages of the journey:

Reshaping: The process of changing your life from one form to another-this is the conditioning stage.

Re-Evaluating: This is part of the assessment process, understanding your current state and the combination of where you've been, where you are and where you want to go.

Restoration: This part is the renewing of the mind, this is the big do-over. The process of conversion of the former and making it new again.

Where are you? Circle one:

Reshaping

Re-evaluation

Restoration

One of the best ways for you to continue to build is making sure your foundation is solid. A strong foundation will help you withstand during the journey.

Taking steps back doesn't always mean decline.
Sometimes you have to step back to get a better view.

The Assessment

What must you tear down in order to move forward?

What can your life experiences do for you?

What are the 3 stages of the journey?

After reading today's lesson, what did you hear?

What are you going to do with the new information you received?

My thoughts… Use this space to write your "Aha" Moments?

DAY 7

WHY?

In everything you do, there is a reason for it, there is a "Why". Everyone's "Why" is different. Your "Why" in life is what you have to discover. It's what wakes you up in the morning and makes you want to get out of bed. Your motivation and your "Why" are similar but are different. What motivates you to do something may be different from the reason why you do something. Your purpose, your passion, and your calling are your "Why" in life, but what motivates you to live it out may be someone or something. For example; your children, your parents, a spouse or a friend could be your motivation to live out your "Why" or even to discover your "Why".

Your "Why" in life is much bigger than a set of daily task and routines. Your "Why" is the reason you were born. I heard it said that there are 2 important days in life, the day you were born and the day you know why. I think the second is just as important as the first, because when you discover it, that's when living really starts to get good. That's when you begin to look at things that motivate you to continue and move in your "Why". You begin to understand why your life has been shaped the way it has been shaped and why you went through some of the things you went through in life. Your "Why" is in direct correlation to the journey you have been traveling your whole life, whether you realize it or not.

Everything that has happened to you and for you are all a part of a bigger picture to move you closer to understanding the very reason you were born. Marian Wright Edelman, the founder of the Children's Defense Fund said: "Service is the rent we pay for living". I also heard someone say: "your talents are God's gift to you, what you do with it is your gift back to Him".

What you do with your life matters. The interesting thing is most people don't think their life matters. As a result, they end up wasting time and not being productive. You will never know what you can do if you don't try to do anything. If you look out at society you will see a lot of wasted talent. If we could only grasp that fact that all lives matter, then we would start living like it. Life truly does have a meaning and if we lead with service and contribution we would begin to see the bigger part of the picture.

But first, we must stop being self serving and think of being more social serving; then we would begin to see the fulfillment and the purpose for living. You will never find fulfillment in just serving yourself. You will only find fulfillment and joy in serving others in the capacity that comes naturally to you. It will be based on your life experiences, your pains and the things that bring you joy. Then you will truly have discovered your "Why" for living. Your "Why" will be found internally, but it must be lived out externally. It is for others to experience and the joy and fulfillment that you will feel from that... is your WHY!

Food For Thought

Use your pain to fuel your purpose then life will be worth the living.

Why?

What's the difference between your "Why" and what motivates you?

What are some key factors in helping you to determine your "Why"?

What will lead you to finding fulfillment?

After reading today's lesson, what did you hear?

What are you going to do with the new information you received?

My thoughts… Use this space to write your "Aha" Moments?

DAY 8

WHO TOLD YOU…

I have a few questions to ask you; "Who told you, you are not good enough?" "Who stole your dreams and who robbed you?" "What has planted seeds in your heart that have now taken root?" What we are dealing with in life is much deeper than we realize. In order for us to move forward, we are going to have to dispel some myths and clear up some untruths.

You may have experienced some traumatic events in your life that have led you to believe some things about yourself. As a result, you may be stuck in a cycle of fear and insecurities that have left you paralyzed in nature. Somewhere along the line, you have taken the things that have happened to you and you have allowed them to be the cornerstone upon what you have hinged life upon. You have begun to base your life around a series of events that have happened to you, and you have allowed those events to define your life.

I want to take a minute to share a little something with you. I know all to well what it's like to think I was not enough or that my life would ever amount to anything based on where I come from and what has happened to me. My mom was 13 years old when she became pregnant with me, I was a victim of sexual abuse at the hands of someone who was supposed to protect me, I was homeless at one point in my life, I was a high school drop and the list goes on. I can continue on with the list of all the things that has happened in my life, but I think you get the point.

I've learned that it's not so much about what has happened to you, but how you respond to what has happened to you. I have come to understand that those things don't define who you are. They can help shape you; and you will develop qualities such as courage, resiliency, and audaciousness through each experience that you can use to serve you. You can salvage pieces from those experience and use them to catapult you to higher heights and deeper depths. What could have destroyed me mentally, emotionally and spiritually, I gave it over to God. He was able to transform my life and take my ashes and trade them in for beauty; He wants to do the same for you.

There are experiences that you have gone through that will forever shape your life and leave scars that are still visible. But through the power of love, healing, and forgiveness you will be able to overcome. Love, healing, and forgiveness are the antidotes for living the life you were destined to live.

Don't let your past destroy your destiny. I read the end of the story and we WIN!! You will win if you don't quit. Your future is still being written; pick up the pen, write a new story line. Don't put a period where God has put a comma. So again I ask you, Who told you that you are not enough? You are more than a Conqueror. You are wonderfully and fearfully made. Believe THAT!!!

Food For Thought

You are changed by what has happened to you, but it does not define you. You define YOU!!

Who Told You...

What qualities will you develop as a result of your life being shaped from the things that may have happened to you?

What is the antidote for living the life you are destined to live?

What can destroy your destiny?

After reading today's lesson, what did you hear?

What are you going to do with the new information you received?

My thoughts... Use this space to write your "Aha" Moments?

DAY 9

LESSONS IN THE MIRROR

The beginning of the healing process starts in the mirror. It starts with you making a conscious decision that you want to heal. This is not a passive thing, this has to be intentional. The reason why most people never heal is because they don't want to do the work in order to heal. Healing requires your full attention and can be a very painful process. It's like you having a broken bone in your body; sometimes they have to continue the break in order to set it back in the proper place. However, once they set it and it heals, it will be stronger than it was before.

Healing is very serious and should not be a task that you go at alone. It can be painful during the breakthrough process. It can be painful because you are breaking through unchartered territories and setting a new course in your life down a road that you have never been on. It is going to be unfamiliar and uncomfortable. You are going to want to run and retreat back to the familiar. I promise if you stay the course you will experience breakthrough and healing in areas of your life you never thought were possible.

When you look in the mirror what do you see? I want you to stop for a moment and get a compact mirror or a hand held mirror preferable because the only area I want you to focus on is your eyes. I want you to stare into your eyes. At first, the person you are looking at will seem unfamiliar to you. Then as you look a little longer you will begin to see the hurt and pain within. As you are looking in the mirror you will begin to cry for the person you are looking at because you are seeing your soul. They say the eyes are the window to the soul. That is where your healing has to take place.

Healing can begin in the form of recognizing the stages: **Truth, Unveiling, and Triggers.**

Truth: What has happened to me that has caused me to feel this way about myself?

Unveiling: Unleashing the hidden secrets that you have buried that has resulted in guilt and shame.

Triggers: The sensitive areas that connect you to your pain.

When you are ready to take a look in the mirror and do the work I recommend you enlist help in the form of a life coach, pastor, counselor, therapist or someone who can help you walk through the journey. Each one can offer you help at different stages of your healing process. When I went on the journey I went alone and God was gracious enough to send me help along the way. I didn't know what the journey entailed. I just knew I no longer wanted to be broken and I was willing to take drastic measures to get my healing. Healing is a crucial part of living out your destiny. "Lessons in the Mirror" is where it truly begins. The journey awaits you...

Food For Thought

Healing
is possible
if you do the
WORK.

Lessons in the Mirror

Where does the healing process take place?

What are the stages of healing?

Who are some people who can help you during the healing process?

After reading today's lesson, what did you hear?

What are you going to do with the new information you received?

My thoughts… Use this space to write your "Aha" Moments?

DAY 10

FORGIVE THAT

Why is there always so much controversy surrounding forgiveness? Why do we have a hard time realizing forgiveness is the key to healing, wholeness and moving forward in life. Forgiveness is lived out in the heart. It is one of those things that if you don't give it affects you in a major way. Part of the reason why we have a hard time forgiving others is because we feel like people don't deserve it. We think it's our responsibility to make people suffer because we've suffered. I'll tell you a secret, "That's not our job."

We think it's our right and duty to withhold forgiveness to someone for something they did to us. While you are angry and holding a grudge the other person is living their life and may not even be thinking about you. Holding a grudge serves no one. Everything is forgivable even if the place of intent was malicious and even if it caused you great harm or damage. The damage you will do to yourself by not forgiving is far worse. For your own well-being you must forgive.

Things didn't really start to change for me until I was able to forgive my abuser. In my mind he did the unthinkable to me and did not deserve to be forgiven, and I held onto it for a long time. It caused me to be angry, bitter and broken. It was only until I began to understand the power of forgiveness that healing was able to take place.

Forgiveness is powerful, but only if you give it away. Forgiveness is a gift you can give yourself and others. You can't withhold it because if you do it looses its power. We must be willing to give it freely. When you give it, it does 2 things:

1. It Frees

2. It Empowers

It frees you from the bondage of allowing the person to have power over you in the form of resentment and bitterness. When you forgive you are in essence taking your power back and no longer allowing those circumstances to control your life. It can also liberate and empower you to let go of all the guilt and shame you have been holding onto so you can stop beating yourself up.

Think of forgiveness as a gift that keeps on giving and you can never run out of it. There is a passage in the Bible in Mathew 18, that says *"we should forgive 70 times 7"*, now that sounds like a crazy number, which equals about 490 times. The number is not the point. The point is that we should forgive as many times as needed. It has been said, not forgiving someone is like you drinking poison and waiting for the other person to die. Not forgiving only hurts you, not the other person. Un-forgiveness keeps you bound and stuck. I think it's time we let freedom reign. Now, Forgive That!!

Food For Thought

Forgiveness frees and empowers. Now go liberate yourself.

Forgive That

If someone was malicious and caused you great harm should you forgive them?

Why should you freely forgive?

Finish the sentence: Forgiveness is _____ but only if you give it away.

After reading today's lesson, what did you hear?

What are you going to do with the new information you received?

My thoughts... Use this space to write your "Aha" Moments?

DAY 11

DEAL AND HEAL

Confrontations are a necessary part of the healing process. In order for you to heal you are going to have to identify those areas in your life that cause you pain and uneasiness. You have to identify your triggers and name them; it is an important part of the healing process. We can not conquer something if we don't confront it and we can't confront what we are not willing to identify. It's equivalent to bringing a knife to a gunfight; you would be ill-equipped for the battle you are fighting. You have to know who your enemy is so you can properly prepare your plan of attack.

An effective healing process is strategic. Suppose you went to the doctor and she asked you what was wrong with you and you kept telling her you didn't know what was wrong; you're just in pain. She continues to ask you a series of questions to try and get more information so she can properly treat you, but you keep crying and you don't give her any information. How can she properly treat you? Are you even at the right doctor? Is it your foot, should you be at the Podiatrist? Is it your heart, should you see a Heart Specialist? Is it your eyes, should you see an Optometrist?

In all of your pain, there are triggers. There are touch points and sensitive areas. They set us off or manifest themselves in many ways as a result of an underlying pain from something that has happened in your life. That's what you have to identify.

Emotions and issues such as rejection, abandonment, insecurity, and trust are as a result of something we have experienced in life. Our triggers typically let us know which one we are dealing with. If you pay attention to the adverse reaction you are having to a particular situation, you will see signs. When a situation arises take a moment while the emotion is still raw to ask yourself a few questions:

1. What am I feeling?

2. Why am I feeling this way?

3. What does this remind me of?

Usually, there is a memory that is associated with the emotion of what you are feeling and that is what you have to trace. When the memory surfaces and comes to the forefront, don't quickly dismiss it. That is the moment when you confront it. You can not change the past, but you can acknowledge it's effect, and deal with it from that point. You must put it in its proper context regarding how it relates to your life now. Is there a lesson associated with it? Is there someone you need to forgive as a result of it? Use the power of forgiveness as your healing ointment so you can finally put it to rest. Deal, so you can Heal.

Food For Thought

Just like broken bones, once it heals it becomes stronger.

Deal and Heal

What must you do with areas in your life that cause you pain and uneasiness?

How do you know what you are dealing with regarding your emotions and what should you pay attention to?

What is usually associated with the emotion of what you are feeling and what do you need to do with it?

After reading today's lesson, what did you hear?

What are you going to do with the new information you received?

My thoughts... Use this space to write your "Aha" Moments?

DAY 12

FREEDOM AIN'T FREE

Everything costs! When you want something in life it is going to cost you something. It's up to you to get the tools necessary to invest in your freedom. Freedom is not always a physical state. Freedom is also in the mind. When you think freedom, you have to think freedom from what? What form of bondage is attached to it? When I think about the transformation journey and going from one state to the next, something has to change. For example, in order for the butterfly to live, the caterpillar had to die. You can not be who you are and who you want to be all at the same time.

There is a transition between transformation. Transformation starts in the mind and it involves a mental shift. Prior to putting action behind anything, you first have to make a decision before the mental process can occur. Before you make a decision you should weigh the pros and cons.

1. How can this serve me?

2. Is this good for me and how can I benefit from it?

3. Am I passionate about it?

4. Can someone else benefit from it through me?

5. Is this part of my life's mission?

You first want to make sure it is worth your time and energy. You will want to count the cost.

During the transition process there is a metamorphosis that is taking place. Things are shedding that you no longer need where you are going. Those things may have served a purpose during one season of your life, but are not necessary for the next season. The journey you are on requires that you do work. It may be in the form of therapy, a rededication of your spiritual beliefs, a re-evaluation of your values or simply purging from old habits that no longer serve you.

Everything costs. All of these things require you to take deliberate steps and counting the cost is necessary for this life altering journey. It is going to require a lot of grit to continue on in the face of adversity. What you are doing is going against the grain. You are trying to free yourself from the bondage of self-sabotage, un-forgiveness and all the insecurities that you have associated with past pains that may have kept you in bondage. So when I tell you freedom ain't free; It ain't! I know it's not proper English, but it just AIN'T. Your healing is going to cost you something, but the rewards are PRICELESS. You just have to ask yourself- Am I willing to pay the price?

Food For Thought

Breaking chains require COURAGE.

Freedom Ain't FREE

Finish the sentence: You can not be who you are and...

Where does transformation start and what has to happen?

What are the different forms of work required on this journey?

After reading today's lesson, what did you hear?

What are you going to do with the new information you received?

My thoughts… Use this space to write your "Aha" Moments?

DAY 13

REMOVE THE BANDAGE

You can't keep walking around with bandages on. You will never heal. My youngest daughter loves bandages. If she as gets a hang nail or if she sees an old scar she is reaching for a bandage. Bandages are a temporary fix. They were designed to help catch the blood from a wound and keep out contaminates so the wound doesn't get infected. When you keep the bandage on too long, it doesn't get any air and it can't heal properly. At some point, you have to take the bandage off so it can breathe and heal.

There is a certain level of comfort in bandages. It gives us a sense that the problem is taken care of and now we can rest. Not true, we can't take what was meant to be a temporary solution and make it a permanent fix. At some point, we are going to have to deal with it. Avoiding things will not make them go away. In fact, it only makes it worse, if left alone it can easily become infected.

I knew a woman who had an injury on her leg that she didn't properly tend to. She kept trying to do home remedies because she was avoiding going to the doctor. She didn't think it was that serious. She thought it was something she could handle. By the time she finally went to the doctor gangrene had set in and they had to amputate her leg.

Avoidance isn't a good thing. We think it will just go away on its own. I wish it was that simple. There are some things in life that you are just going to have to tend to. They are going to need your attention and a little TLC (Tender Loving Care). What I find interesting is that most people will do things for other people that they won't even do for themselves. They will nurse a loved one, they will make sure their significant others and children are taken care of and put themselves on the back burner. Then one day they look up and wonder where the time has gone or they've experiencing burn out and fatigue. Even in the process of taking care of others what you are subliminally doing is avoiding you. You get so busy helping everybody else that you neglect you. Everyone knows who to call when they need help and you will be right there for them. But who do you call?

The only way healing is going to take place is if you are intentional. You have to be intentional and specific about what you need. It's interesting how much time we spend on our outer appearance. What if we devoted the same amount of time to our personal development and growth? For example, if you spend about 2-4 hours at a place of grooming every other week, try matching your internal growth with that. You would see a big difference in your life. What you put on will fade, but what you put in you is a seed that will continue to harvest if you nurture it. Remove the bandages, no more temporary fixes, just go all IN!

Food For Thought

The longer
you leave a bandage
on, the harder
it is to get off; the
separation
of it will be just as
painful.

Remove the Bandage

What happens when you avoid things?

What are some things you experience as a result of not taking care of yourself?

Healing can only take place if you are what?

After reading today's lesson, what did you hear?

What are you going to do with the new information you received?

My thoughts... Use this space to write your "Aha" Moments?

DAY 14

JUST WALK AWAY

It takes courage to just walk away. You can not be who you are and who you want to be at the same time. Saying good bye is never easy but it is sometimes necessary. There is an unhealthy relationship that you may have developed with yourself a long time ago that hasn't allowed you to reach your full potential. There are things that have happened to you that robbed you from operating out of your higher self and developing into the person you were born to be.

Today I want to invite you to take a different approach on how you live life. There are stories you have been telling yourself that has limited your potential. You were born for a specific reason, at a specific time and for a specific task. You are the answer to someone's questions. You are the relief to a problem. Your life has so much meaning and someone is waiting for you.

I want you to think about the fact that your passions, your gifts, and talents are all aligned with your assignment on earth which is your life's mission. We all have one, yet some of us have abandoned our life's mission because we never really understood it or thought we were unworthy of it. Some of us never realized our life mattered. Many of us look at how we were conceived and think we were an accident.

It doesn't matter how you were conceived. God knew who you were going to be and He gave you an assignment to fulfill on earth. We have allowed the problems and the cares of this world to diminish our value and self-worth. In order for you to embrace the new you, you are going to have to walk away from your old thinking, your old belief system and develop a new one. I am going to need you to believe in yourself like never before. If you have never read the book of Genesis in the Bible, I would urge you to read chapter 1 verses 26-27, to know whose image you are made in.

This is not about religion or a question of what your spiritual beliefs are, it is a statement to emphasize that no one is an accident. Everything created serves a purpose and so do you. So many times we base our living on what has happened to us. When traumatic experiences happen, we allow those things to flip our world upside down, and yes sometimes it does. But what has happened to you does not define who you are. I know that you can't undo what has happened, but you can acknowledge the effects of it and not allow it to define your entire life. Don't take a moment of your life and make it the sum total of your whole life. Your story is still being written, you're still up for the leading role, there is no understudy for you. Only you can play your role the way it needs to be played. Only you can live the life you were destined to live. Make a decision to leave who you were for the person you need to be in order to live the life you were destined to live. Just walk away from the old and embrace the NEW!

Food For Thought

How something is made
isn't as important as
why it was made.
It will still
serve
its purpose.

Just Walk Away

What has limited your potential?

How can you embrace the new you?

If you can't undo what has happened to you, what can you do?

After reading today's lesson, what did you hear?

What are you going to do with the new information you received?

My thoughts… Use this space to write your "Aha" Moments?

DAY 15

CONFIDENCE

Brokenness can steal your confidence. It will leave you feeling like you are unworthy and have nothing to offer. Confidence is the very thing you need to move forward and fulfill the plans that are on your life. If you find yourself lacking the confidence to do the things that are set in your heart; it is because fear and doubt have crept in. Confidence is already in you, you have just allowed doubt to overrule it. You may have allowed things that have happened to you steal your confidence.

When I began to understand how broken I was and that I could not trust my emotions because they were fleeting, I knew I had to draw from another source that was much greater than me. I began to put my trust and faith in God. All I kept thinking about was if all I had to rely on was myself then I am done. I was at the end of my rope. I knew there had to be more so I began to call on a source higher than me.

I knew prayer was talking to God. I had always heard of Him and I grew up in church, but I didn't really have a relationship with Him. I needed to know if He was real for myself. I began to pray and cry and tell him everything I was feeling; all my fears, all my anxieties, and my concerns. I asked a bunch of questions; why did this happen and why did that happen, and

I told him how angry I was and that it wasn't fair. This went on for months, I was at a point of desperation. I had cried all I could cry and one day I remembered my tears were no longer tears but quiet solemn moments where I reflected on my life's journey. Before I was only looking at it from my angle and was only concerned about what happened to me.

God began to give me a different perspective. I was able to see all the players in each scenario and put myself in their shoes. Suddenly I began to see their pain and things started to become more clear to me. I discovered the keys to my healing were in me all along. It was the love of God that dwelled in me and my heart was opened. The memory of things that happened to me didn't go away but I began to learn the power of forgiveness and I allowed healing to take place in my heart. It was only at that point I was able to stand confidently as the woman I was created to be.

Confidence and brokenness can not exist together. Just like faith and fear can't operate in the same space. You will have one or the other. The confidence I have is because of the God in me, from whom I draw my strength from. God is what sustains me and allows me to continue on the journey that has been purposed for me. I don't know where your journey is leading you, but if you have faith and trust the process of forgiveness and healing, then your confidence will be restored and you will begin to see the plans unfold.

Food For Thought

You hold the keys to what you are looking for.

Confidence

What can steal your confidence?

What is prayer?

How can your confidence be restored?

After reading today's lesson, what did you hear?

What are you going to do with the new information you received?

My thoughts… Use this space to write your "Aha" Moments?

DAY 16

YOU DESERVE

Did you know that you deserve to live an amazing life? It doesn't matter what you've done or what you have been through. It doesn't matter who supported you or who didn't. It doesn't matter if no one ever acknowledged a thing you've done. Know that you deserve to live a life free from stress, worry, anger, depression or any other thing you can conjure up.

You deserve a break! You deserve to take a few deep breaths and realize that you have made it this far in the journey and I want to commend you for that. You deserve to smile, you deserve to be happy and you deserve joy in your life.

Sometimes we are waiting for situations to change around us and we are the ones that have to change. Situations and people may stay the same but you can be the change in the equation. In life, there is always going to be something going on. But you don't have to allow it to take you away from your peace. You always have to tuck a piece of your peace away in your heart. So that when things arise, it doesn't move you from your peace. You deal with things as needed, make your response your responsibility and allow others to take ownership for theirs.

In order to truly live the life you deserve you are going to have to see things for what they are. The good, the bad and the ugly and still hold onto your peace. There will come a day when you will look at your life and realize that there was no turmoil or drama and you will say "Today was a good day." Now the key is learning how to rest in that. I want this day to be a day where you come out of mourning and enter into the marvelous light. For the past 15 days, you have been digging deep. You've been doing the work, you have been reflecting, focusing, telling the truth, forgiving, and working on your healing.

There is a life that is rich and fulfilling that is waiting for you. You just have to go get it. The only way you are going to get to "You Deserve" is if you say it to yourself, "I Deserve…" In order to get to that, you have to have a selfish moment and turn all your focus and attention to yourself and TAKE IT!!

I know you have been through a lot in your life, but I want to tell you that you really deserve to have peace on earth. You deserve to smile and you deserve to be free. You deserve to live the life that God has destined for you to live. It doesn't matter what they told you, you are worthy, you are more than enough and you deserve to live a fulfilling life that is full of joy, unspeakable joy. Yes, You Deserve It!!

Food For Thought

There is a rich, full life waiting for you, you DESERVE it!!

You Deserve a Break Today

** You should go for a walk or take a nice long bubble bath. ☺

After reading today's lesson, what did you hear?

What are you going to do with the new information you received?

My thoughts… Use this space to write your "Aha" Moments?

DAY 17

FOR I KNOW THE PLANS

"For I know the plans I have for you…" I remember always hearing that quoted and wondered, "Well, tell me the plans, so I can know them"(in my sarcastic voice). Then I came to realize it is not that simple. In one of my favorite books, The Alchemist there was a boy in search of his personal legend, which is what we call our purpose. Throughout the entire book, he went on many different journeys, some of them seem to take him in a round about way. During the story, he went through much turmoil but in the end he discovered his legend. I'm not going to give you any other details, I don't want to ruin the joy of you reading the book. It is a very good read and it is packed with so much wisdom and great insight. On occasions I still re-read it for inspiration, especially my highlighted notes.

This is the definition the Author, Paulo Coelho used in "The Alchemist" to describe a personal legend:

"It is God's blessing, it is the path that God chose for you here on Earth. Whenever we do something that fills us with enthusiasm, we are following our legend. However, we don't all have the courage to confront our own dream". He talks about how we know what we want to do but are afraid of hurting those around us by abandoning everything to pursue our dreams.

I remember times when I would hold back on what I wanted to do because my loved ones didn't understand or support my dreams. It kept me in a shell, feeling sad, isolated and lonely. I knew if I was going to pursue my personal legend I had to break free of what everyone else thought I should do or be. I had to do what was in my heart. I had to pursue my "I AM" and I had to tell myself and affirm within me all the things I knew I was. I am great, I am more than a conqueror, I am a teacher, I am a great woman of character, I am prosperous and most of all- I AM HEALED! I had to speak my truth about who I was and all the dreams and ambitions that were in me. That was the beginning of my liberty; declaring and standing in my true 'I AM" and allowing myself to dream again.

You have to make a decision to pursue the plans for your life. Yes, there are plans for your life, and it starts with acknowledging your dreams and declaring your "I Am". No one else can live your personal legend for you. It is yours, it will be what wakes you up in the morning, but it will also be what keeps you up at night. You will become obsessed with the pursuit of it because it is what will bring you satisfaction. And once you are made aware of it, it will become the air you breathe. If you don't pursue it, it will feel like you can't breath and all the air is being sucked out of your lungs. The only thing that will fill it back up is Purpose, Peace, and the Power to be exactly who you were created to be. There are plans for your life, take a deep breath, now exhale and GO PURSUE it!

Food For Thought

"It's the possibility of making the dream come true that makes life interesting."

Paulo Coelho

For I Know the Plans

What is a personal legend?

Who can live your personal legend for you?

Why is it that some people don't follow their personal legend?

After reading today's lesson, what did you hear?

What are you going to do with the new information you received?

My thoughts… Use this space to write your "Aha" Moments?

DAY 18

LACK NO MORE

You have everything you need to do what you have been called to do. You have not because you ask not. I worked with a woman who made everything seem so simple. If we have to do something and we don't at first appear to have the tools or the resources, she would say "Ask God." At first I was like, "duh!" Why didn't I think of that? It didn't matter what I asked her, she would always say "Ask God" and at first it was renewing and refreshing to my faith to be reminded that all we had to do was "Ask God".

But then one day something different happened, I think she said it to me on the wrong day; a day when I wasn't in an ask God mood, and secretly I was annoyed and frustrated. She always said it in such a matter of fact type of way. It just rolled off her tongue effortlessly while giving me a smug look; like I thought I told you this already. The problem I had was she always made it seem so simple. Nothing in my life was ever simple for me, and I was taught that everything I needed I had to work for it and no one was going to give me anything. So I would hear her but it still wasn't real to me.

Then I realized it was nothing wrong with O.T. That's what I would call her Older Towanda, because she's much older than me and she reminds me of what I would be like when I get older. Not asking and rejection are linked together. Everything starts somewhere; it has a root. My mom was a young mom and she did the best she knew how to do raising her children. When you are a child and you ask for things and you are constantly being told no you begin to be afraid of "The Ask" because you don't like how it feels. It is your first encounter with rejection. After hearing no so many times you stop asking and you stop expecting out of fear of being rejected.

You make vows to yourself that when you get older and start working for what you want you will not ask anyone for anything. As I am older I understand that my mom couldn't give me what she didn't have and that her telling me no was not her rejecting me. Sometimes what I wanted I didn't need anyway. I had the wrong view of "The Ask". "The Ask" is also about timing. It may not be the right time to receive what you are asking for. A 5-year-old kid asking for a car is definitely a no. The problem is, the wrong mindset had developed around me asking. So now I am learning to "Ask God" as O.T. would say.

Asking is also having faith, trusting and believing. I have been sharing this simple truth with my friends. Even when we need a parking space they'll say, "Towanda -Ask God". We have not, truly and simply, because we ask not!! Start asking, and then believe and you shall receive. Let there be lack no more, mentally, spiritually, or physically. Whatever you need, "Ask God". You will be surprised by the forms in which your help will come. Just know, it's not always going to look like what you think it should.

My new motto #ASKGOD

Food For Thought

Being told no about something is not a rejection of your character. You are LOVED.

Lack No More

Not asking is linked to what?

What can happen as a result of continually being told no?

Fill in the blanks: Asking is also having: (Name the three things)

_____, _____, _____

After reading today's lesson, what did you hear?

What are you going to do with the new information you received?

My thoughts… Use this space to write your "Aha" Moments?

DAY 19

LIVE OUT LOUD

No more shrinking back! I think Marianne Williamson said it best. *"It's our light, not our darkness that most frighten us."* Think about it, why would our light frighten us? For some of us, it's the part we connect with the least. Everyone always talks about the darkness and their fear of it. Even as a child there is always this thing about being in the dark and we want a night light on. We want a light on because we recognize the illumination of the light, but we have yet to understand the power of it.

In the light is where your power is. The light is where you shine the brightest. The interesting thing about light is you only need a little of it to dispel darkness. Only light can drive out darkness. Over the past few weeks, we have gone to some dark places during this journey; because we were searching for the light at the end of the tunnel. Well, guess what? The light is here, and as the kids would say "It's TURN up time!!!" Yes, it's time to turn up that light and show the world what you are working with. It's time to Live out Loud and let all your goodness shine through.

It's time to unleash your creativity and all the gifts you've been hiding that you only allow a select few to see. Everyone is always talking about all the negative things going on in the world and how darkness is taking over. If we would understand the power of shining our light for the world to see, we could use our gifts to eradicate a lot of what's going on in the world. You are the answer to someone's question. You hold the solution to a problem. Within your pain and struggle is the antidote, you hold the serum and cure within for someone else.

Your joy is in shining your light. It's in your purpose and, it's in your passion. You have the power to Live Out Loud, but you have to exercise that right and stop shrinking back. If the truth is told, you are the only one that is holding you back. Quiet the noise and the chatter that is going on in your head, get a different tune and change the channel. You may need to change your circle. Get around some other people who are shining their light and watch how infectious it is. It only makes you want to shine your light also. I think it's time! Don't you? You've been crying long enough. It's time to wipe those tears away and start rejoicing. Rejoicing for the new season of your life that you are entering in.

Get the information you need to get and learn what you need to learn in order to walk it out. New information will change your life. It will open your mind to a new awareness and you will begin to see things differently. Turn that frown upside down and give it away. Watch how it will make you feel. Put on some bright colors, take off those dark mourning colors, put a pep in your step and Live Out Loud. As you liberate yourself, you unconsciously give others permission to do the same. Your energy will be INFECTIOUS!

(LOL- Live Out Loud) #LIVEOUTLOUD

Food For Thought

When you add
your light
to the world
it makes it
brighter.

Live Out Loud

What most frightens us?

Where is your power?

What will new information do for you?

After reading today's lesson, what did you hear?

What are you going to do with the new information you received?

My thoughts… Use this space to write your "Aha" Moments?

DAY 20

"AHA"

"Aha's" are those sneaky moments that arrest and grab your understanding dead in its tracks. It is the moment where a word was spoken that whispers in your spirit and offers you a nugget of insight . It is a true light bulb moment. It is revelation that causes you to pause and reflect on what was just spoken.

It is you having an encounter with a word that can help change the course of the direction for your life. That was the goal of the *21 Day Transformation Journey*. I wanted you to have a series of "Aha" moments and revelations that would break up your normal pattern. It would provide a shift that goes against the grain and interrupts the stories that have kept you stuck in certain areas. The goal was to allow you an opportunity to stop and have time to reflect and make a decision about where you are in life. It was designed to be a starting point to guide you at the fork in the road of life's many journeys.

The fork is there for a reason it's a point when you must make a decision. Most people don't choose because of fear of the unknown or their indecisiveness. They build a tent at the fork and some go as far as building houses there. The very nature of the word indecisive means not having or showing the ability to make a decision quickly or effectively. But at the core of not making a decision is a decision in itself; it is deciding to not move forward.

No matter what you choose on this journey, there will be obstacles. Facing an obstacle in the road doesn't mean you have not chosen properly. It doesn't necessarily mean you should retreat and run back to take the other road. Sometimes obstacles are there to strengthen you for the journey ahead. The 21-Day Journey was designed to help set you up and prepare you to go deeper in the transformation of your mind. If you listen to that still small voice within, learn to trust your instincts and use the power of prayer ,you will get to where you need to be on this journey.

"Aha" moment are like tokens that you use on life's journeys to pay the toll during those moments of fear, indecisiveness, and obstacles. You store your "Aha" moments in your heart until you need them. They are nuggets; gems that have been dropped on you along the way to make life a little easier while you are traveling to your destination. I love "Aha" moments because I know that I have just received a jewel that will soon serve me or something I can pass along to someone else.

There is more for you on this road, soak up what you need to for the journey, pack light and save room for the gems you will pick up along the way.

Food For Thought

Encouraging words are nourishment for the soul.

Eat Up!

"AHA"

What are "Aha" moments?

Why don't some people make a choice at the fork in the road?

What was the **21 Day Transformation Journey** designed do?

After reading today's lesson, what did you hear?

What are you going to do with the new information you received?

My thoughts… Use this space to write your "Aha" Moments?

DAY 21

"I GOT A NEW ATTITUDE"

It's day 21! Can you believe it? It has been 21 days of me talking in your ear (lol). I hope the time has been fruitful for you. Well, today is the day that you fully clothe yourself in your "New Attitude". Let's make this day symbolic of the journey you went on.

On this day_____(insert today's date) I _____ (Insert Name) completed all 21 Days of the Transformation Journey and I have a "New Attitude"

I know there were days that spoke to you more than others, depending on where you are on your journey. I love when I complete something, it always gives me a reason to celebrate. Sometimes you just have to celebrate yourself instead of waiting for others. So many times we are looking for others to celebrate and acknowledge what we've done. That is not always going to be the case.

Today I want you to take the stance and position that I can do this. There are things you want to do in life and now is the time to do them. For the past 21 days, I have been giving you new information, confirmations and some Aha moments that will help you on your journey. I know you are thinking, has it been 21 days already? Now what? Now is when you really start to put into practice what we have been discussing, now is when you really start to look at the foundation of your life with a "New Attitude." Getting a "New Attitude" is a new realization. I love when I get a "New Attitude" because either I'm so over it, or I'm so excited about it. Which one are you right now? I hope the latter.

I have a challenge for you. I know this may be hard for some of you, but consider going on a 21-day social media fast. During the fast refrain from all social media outlets and journal your thoughts for 21 days. All those things you would consider posting, write it in your journal and talk it out with yourself. (P.S. I talk to myself all the time.) You will be amazed at how clear and organic your thoughts will be.

Go back and re-read your "Aha" moments and decide how you can implement them in your life. What small changes can you make that will have a major impact in your life? What's going to help you on this journey now is momentum and going in for the long haul. Pace yourself, it's a marathon, not a sprint. Take one day at a time. None of this matters if you don't use the information you received and make it applicable in your life. Maya Angelou said *"When you know better, you do better"*. However, my friend Eddie said, "that's not true because there are many things we know we shouldn't do and yet we still do them". I say, when you put action behind that knowing, that's when change can occur.

You hold the keys,
you hold the power;
you've had it all along.

ABOUT THE AUTHOR

Towanda is a wife to Roger and a mother to Kari and Kayla, who are the loves of her life. Healing has become the hallmark of Towanda's life. After experiencing many traumatic experiences in life, she was able to turn her tragedy into triumph. Through various outlets she takes others on the journey to transformation and healing through the power of forgiveness.

To connect with Towanda McEachern
visit **www.towandam.com**

Made in the USA
Middletown, DE
28 February 2024

50471483R00064